Unit 1

1. Make sure kids know their own names and how to ask to go to the bathroom.
2. Review the numbers and do the listening test while students do the next page.

1	2	3
4	5	6
7	8	9
10		

Listening Test

Can the student point to the number the teacher says?

Sign or Stamp

Students can work on this while you test them one-on-one on the previous page.

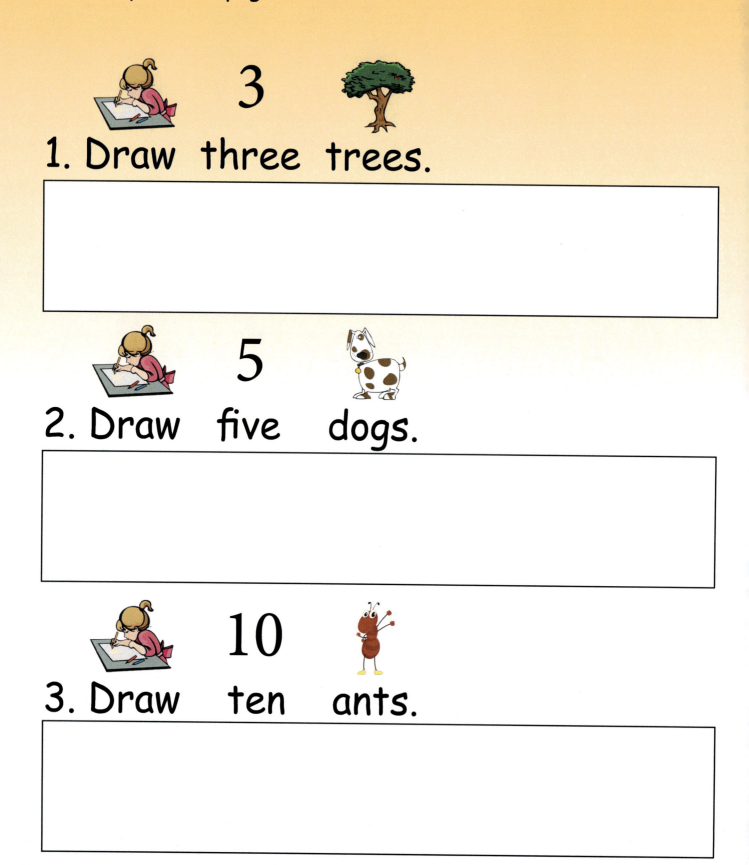

1. Draw three trees.

2. Draw five dogs.

3. Draw ten ants.

Practice the conversation a lot. Students cannot read this yet, so you don't need to ask them to.

Go around and have this conversation with five other students.

When the student can have the conversation one-on-one with you:

Sign or Stamp

Students can work on this while you test them one on one on the previous page.

Name:

Name:

Name:

Name:

Name:

Draw yourself

Your favorite food

Teach and practice the sentences. Then test the students one-on-one.

1.
Sit down, please.

2.
Stand up, please.

3.
Push in your chair.

4.
Walk, please.

5.
Line up. Don't push.

6.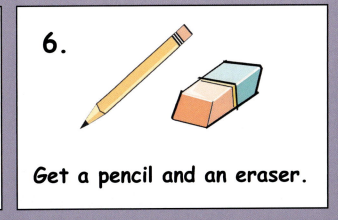
Get a pencil and an eraser.

Listening Test

When the student can understand these commands individually using only listening without gestures of any kind, the teacher can sign.

Sign or Stamp

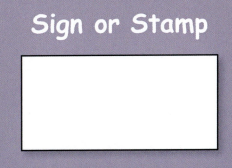

Students can work on this while the teacher tests students one-on-one on the previous page.

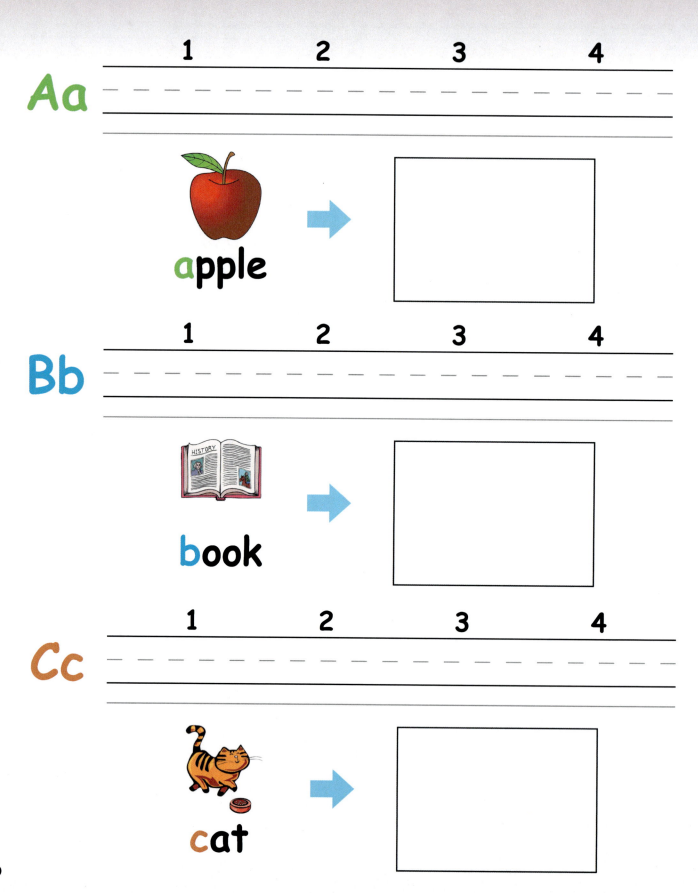

Unit 2

Speaking Practice
Students should be able to communicate when they need something.

I need a _____, please.

1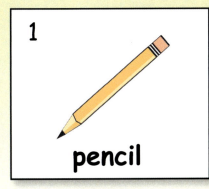
pencil

2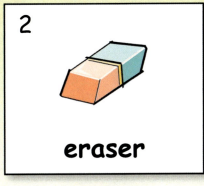
eraser

3
chair

4
book

5
school bag

Listening Practice
Practice as a class and then ask each student individually without any gestures. Sign or stamp when the student can respond correctly to all of the questions or commands.

1. How are you?
2. Where is your book?
3. What is your name?
4. Where is your pencil?
5. Where is your chair?
6. Where is your eraser?

Sign or Stamp

Students can work on this while you test them one on one on the previous page.

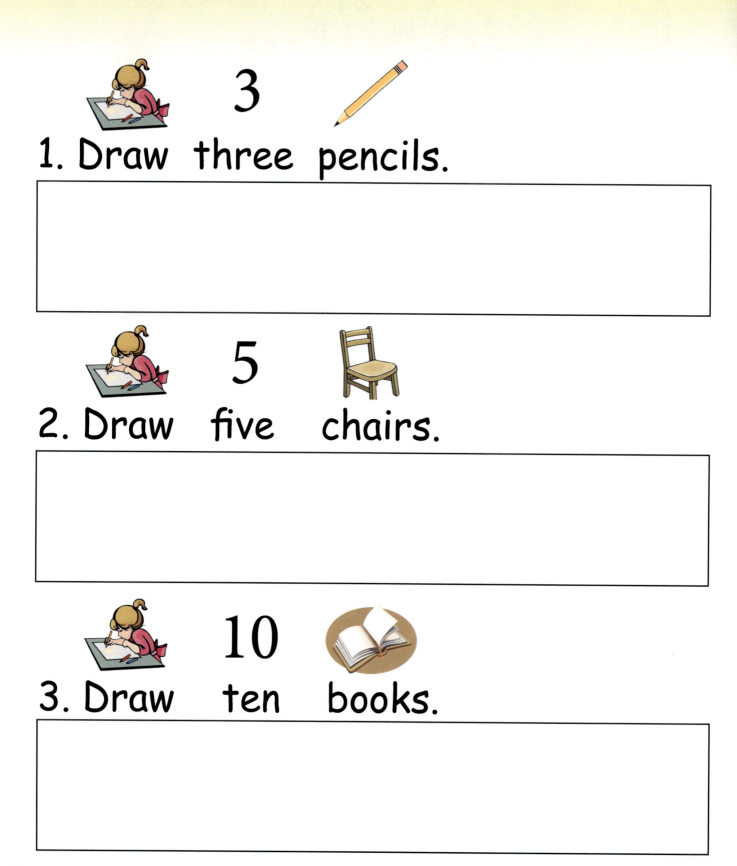

1. Draw three pencils.

2. Draw five chairs.

3. Draw ten books.

Practice lots together. The goal is that students can remember the names and sounds easily even when the letters are mixed up.

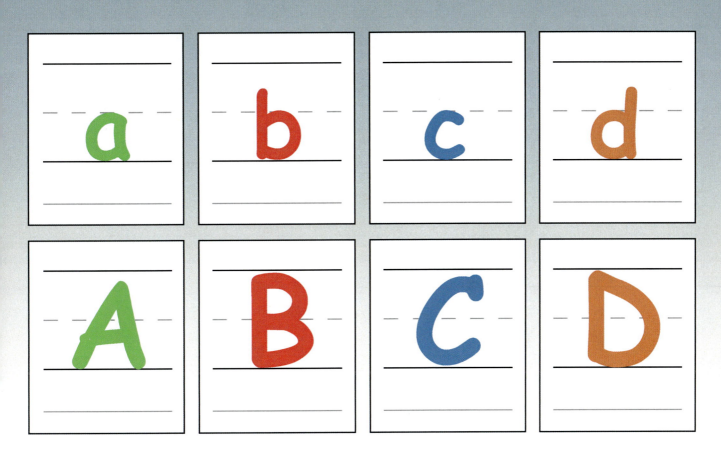

Letter and Sound Recognition

Only sign or stamp when the student can do this on their own! If they can't, have them keep practicing. It's only going to get harder as letters are added.

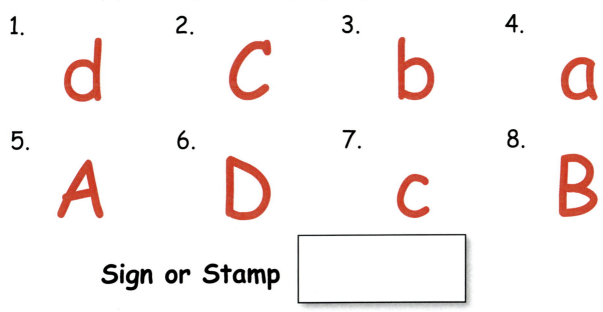

Sign or Stamp

Students can work on this while you test them one on one on the previous page.

        1   2   3   4

Bb

bag →

        1   2   3   4

Cc

cup →

        1   2   3   4

Dd

dog →

Practice lots together. The goal is that students can remember the names and sounds easily even when the letters are mixed up.

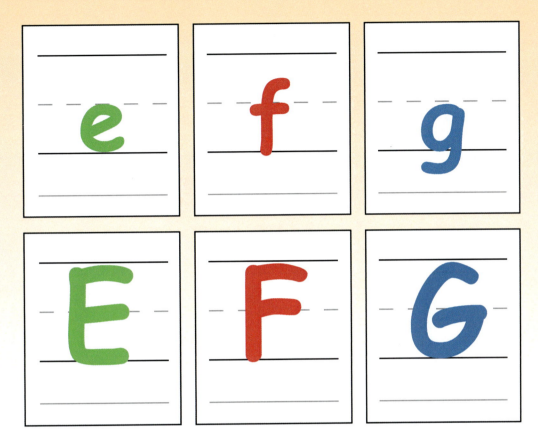

Letter and Sound Recognition

Only sign or stamp when the student can do this on their own! If they can't, have them keep practicing. It's only going to get harder as letters are added.

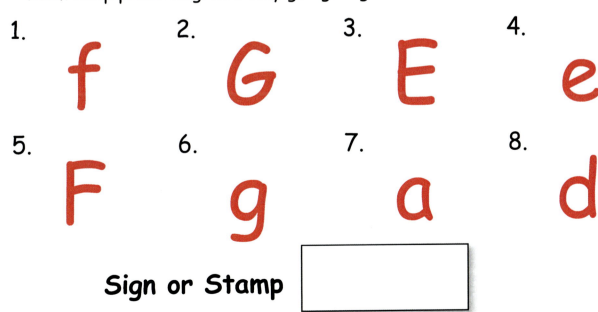

Sign or Stamp

Students can work on this while you test them one on one on the previous page.

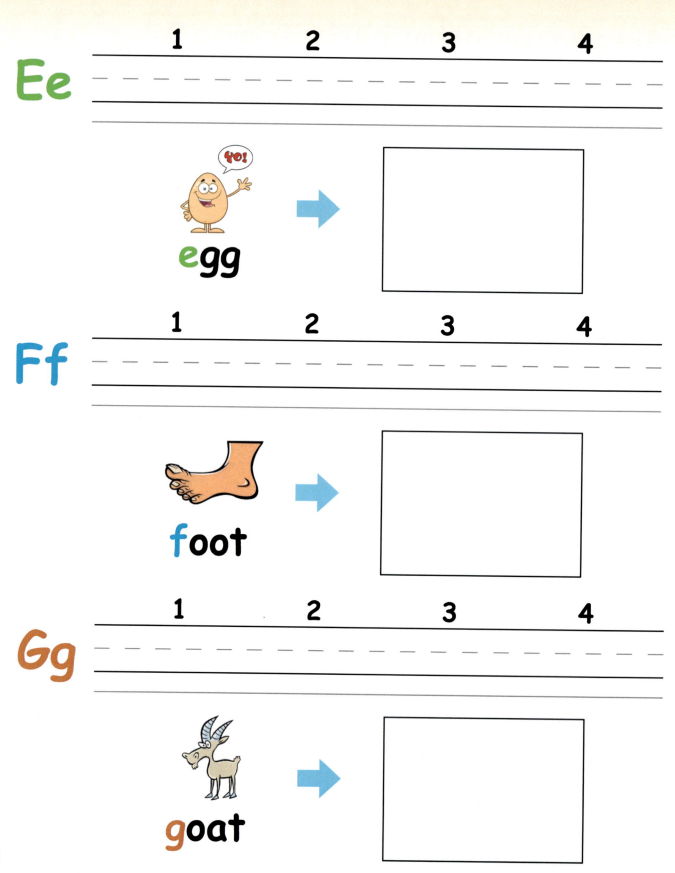

Unit 3

Common Classroom English

Students should be able to understand these individually without gestures. Teach the students to solve problems using paper scissors stone.

1  Sit properly.	2  Look at me, please.	3  Don't fight, please.
4  Paper, scissors, stone.	5  Listen, please.	6  I'm going to count down from five.

Listening Practice

Practice as a class and then ask each student individually without any gestures. Sign or stamp when the student can respond correctly to all of the questions or commands.

1. Sit properly.
2. Don't fight, please. What do you do?
3. Look at me, please.
4. What is this? (eraser, pencil...)

Sign or Stamp

Students can work on this while you test them one on one on the previous page.

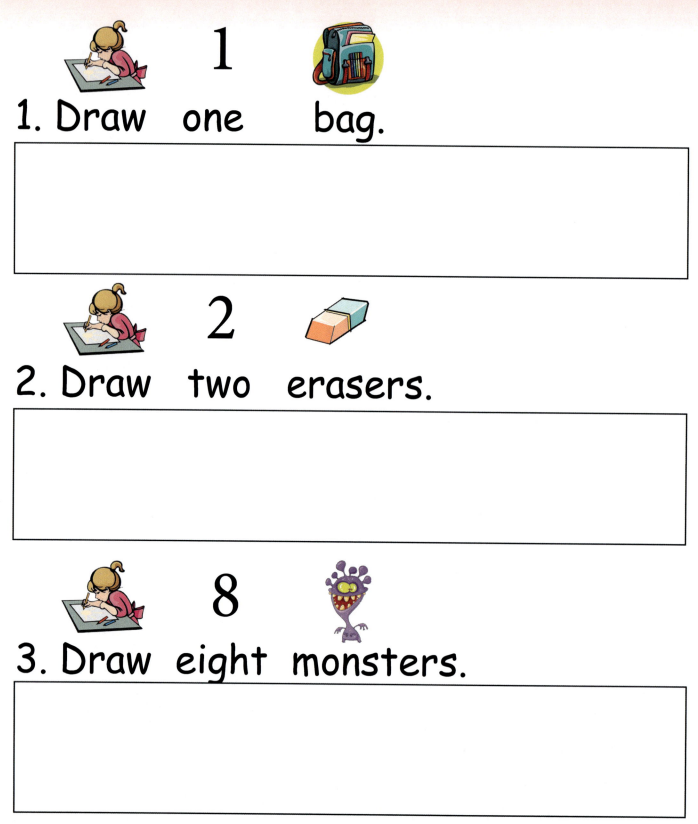

1. Draw one bag.

2. Draw two erasers.

3. Draw eight monsters.

Practice lots together. The goal is that students can remember the names and sounds easily even when the letters are mixed up.

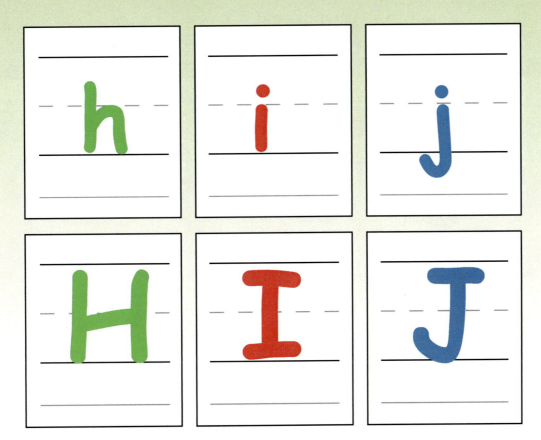

Letter and Sound Recognition

Only sign or stamp when the student can do this on their own! If they can't, have them keep practicing. It's only going to get harder as letters are added.

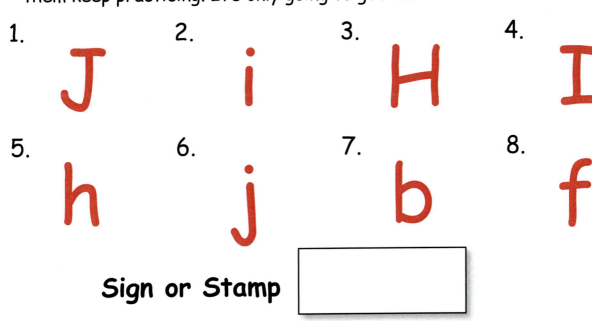

Sign or Stamp

Students can work on this while you test them one on one on the previous page.

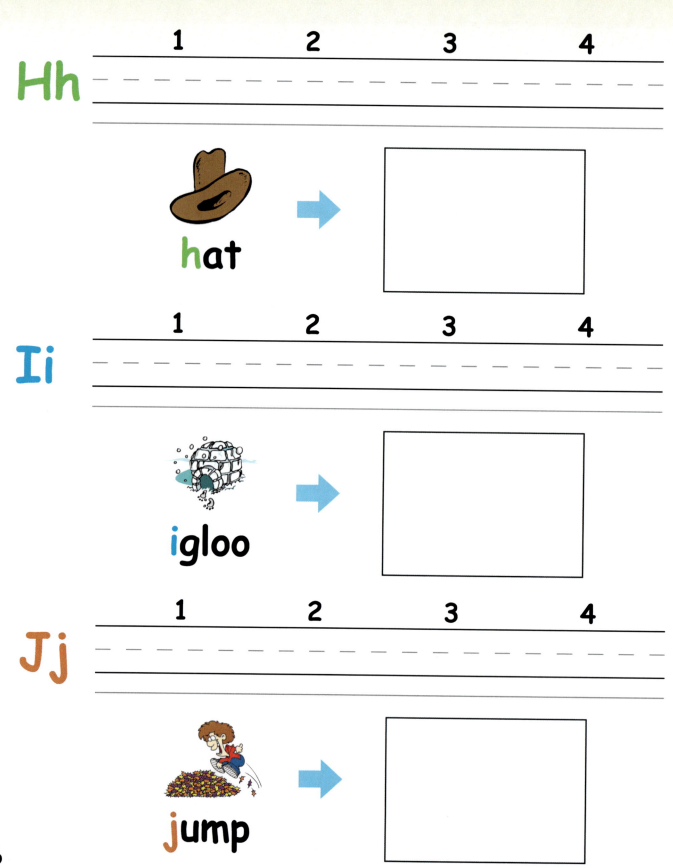

Practice lots together. The goal is that students can remember the names and sounds easily even when the letters are mixed up.

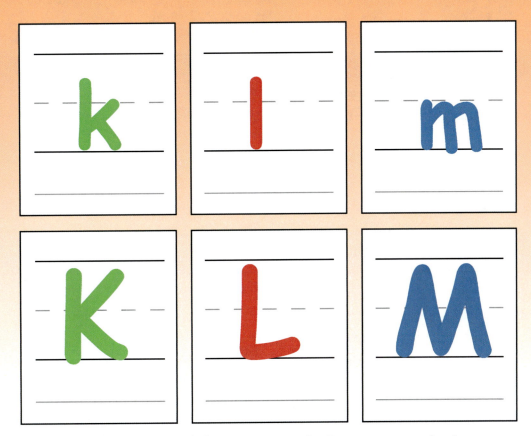

Letter and Sound Recognition

Only sign or stamp when the student can do this on their own! If they can't, have them keep practicing. It's only going to get harder as letters are added.

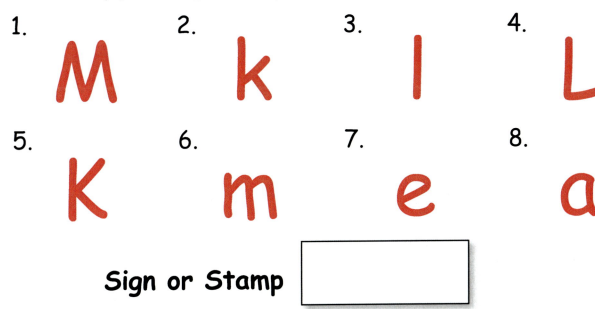

Sign or Stamp

Students can work on this while you test them one on one on the previous page.

Kk   1   2   3   4

kick →

Ll   1   2   3   4

light →

Mm   1   2   3   4

mad →

Unit 4

Common Classroom English

Students should be able to understand and say these individually without help.

1  May I go to the bathroom, please?	2 	3 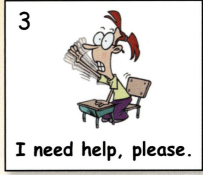 I need help, please.
4  He took my <u>pencil</u>.	5  Look at this!	6  I am done.

Listening Practice

Practice as a class and then ask each student individually without any gestures. Sign or stamp when the student can respond correctly to all of the questions or commands.

1. How are you?
2. What is your name?
3. Go get a pencil and eraser, please.
4. Look at me, please.
5. Turn to page five.

Sign or Stamp

1. Understand the sentences. 2. Remember the words.
3. Color the pictures.

1. Color the tiger.

2. Color the lion.

3. Color the monkey.

4. Color the giraffe.

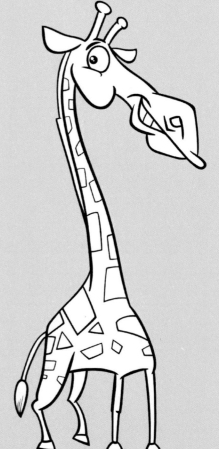

5. Color the hippo.

Practice lots together. The goal is that students can remember the names and sounds easily even when the letters are mixed up.

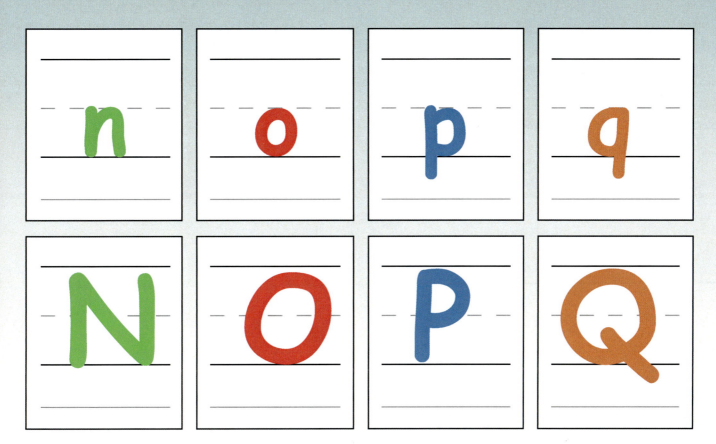

Letter and Sound Recognition

Only sign or stamp when the student can do this on their own! If they can't, have them keep practicing. It's only going to get harder as letters are added.

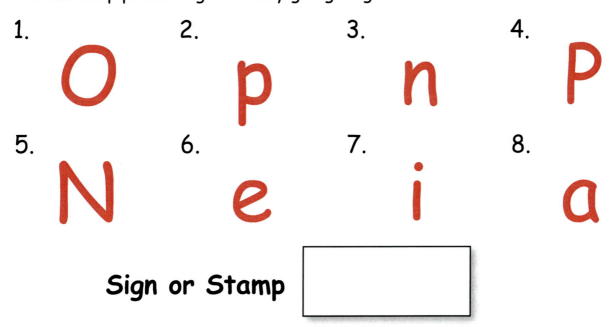

Sign or Stamp

Students can work on this while you test them one on one on the previous page.

Nn

1   2   3   4

net

Oo

1   2   3   4

on

Pp

1   2   3   4

pig

Practice lots together. The goal is that students can remember the names and sounds easily even when the letters are mixed up.

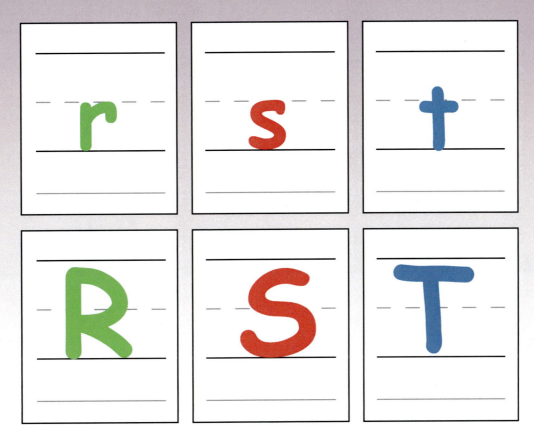

Letter and Sound Recognition

Only sign or stamp when the student can do this on their own! If they can't, have them keep practicing. It's only going to get harder as letters are added.

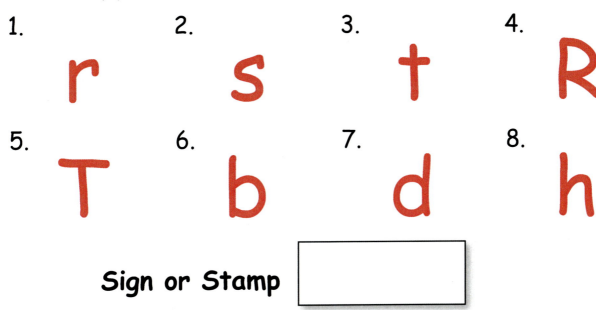

Sign or Stamp

Students can work on this while you test them one on one on the previous page.

Rr   1   2   3   4

red →

Ss   1   2   3   4

sit →

Tt   1   2   3   4

tag →

Review Assessments

A. Speaking

1. Practice as a class and in partners beforehand.
2. How many sentences can you make in a minute?

1.
2.
3.
4.

5.
6.
7.
8.

9.
10.
11.

Review Assessments

B. Reading

How many letters and sounds can the student do in a minute? (Start over at 1 if the student finishes the list before a minute has passed.)

1.	2.	3.	4.	5.	6.	7.	8.
c	e	t	i	f	p	l	b
9.	10.	11.	12.	13.	14.	15.	16.
r	b	d	a	g	k	m	p
17.	18.	19.	20.	21.	22.	23.	24.
n	h	j	o	q	s	l	a

C. Listening

Ask each student individually without gestures of any kind. How many questions out of the total does the student respond correctly to?

1. How are you?
2. What is your name?
3. Go get a pencil and eraser, please.
4. Look at me, please.
5. Where is your textbook?
6. Turn to page five.
7. Where is your pencil.
8. Sit properly, please.
9. Don't fight, please. What do you do?

D. Vocabulary

See how many words the student can remember out of the total.

26

Unit 5

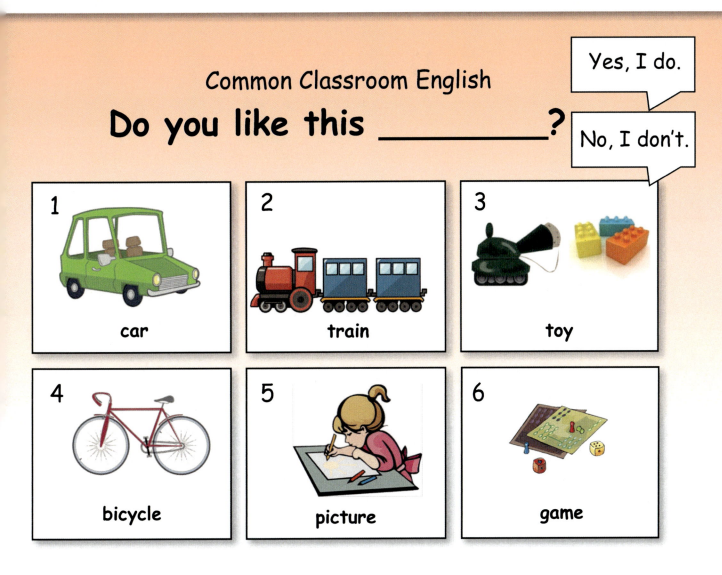

Listening Practice

Practice as a class and then ask each student individually without any gestures. Sign or stamp when the student can respond correctly to all of the questions or commands.

1. Where is the car?
2. What is your name?
3. Where is the toy?
4. What is this?

Sign or Stamp

1. Understand the sentences. 2. Remember the words.
3. Color the pictures.

1. Color the toy.

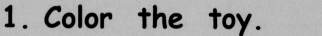

2. Color the train.

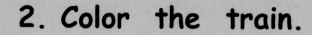

3. Color the picture.

4. Color the car.

Practice lots together. The goal is that students can remember the names and sounds easily even when the letters are mixed up.

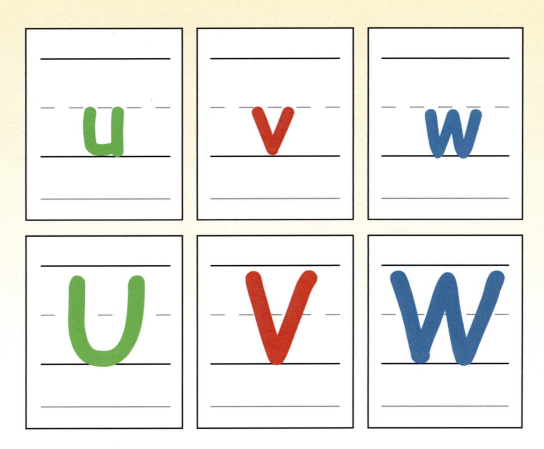

Letter and Sound Recognition

Only sign or stamp when the student can do this on their own! If they can't, have them keep practicing. It's only going to get harder as letters are added.

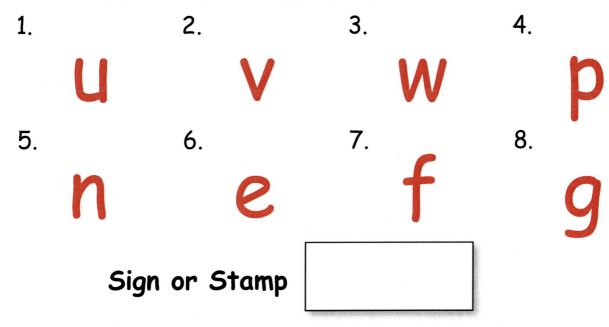

Sign or Stamp

Students can work on this while you test them one on one on the previous page.

　　　　　1　　　　2　　　　3　　　　4

Uu

up →

　　　　　1　　　　2　　　　3　　　　4

Vv

vet →

　　　　　1　　　　2　　　　3　　　　4

Ww

wig →

Practice lots together. The goal is that students can remember the names and sounds easily even when the letters are mixed up.

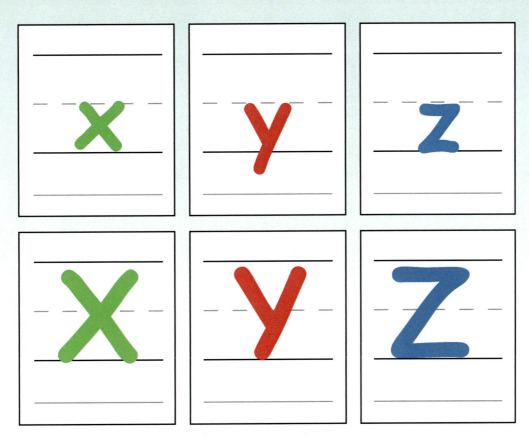

Letter and Sound Recognition

Only sign or stamp when the student can do this on their own! If they can't, have them keep practicing. It's only going to get harder as letters are added.

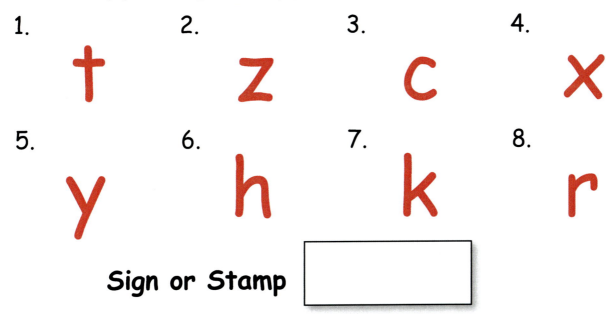

Sign or Stamp

Students can work on this while you test them one on one on the previous page.

Aa Bb Cc Dd Ee Ff Gg

Hh Ii Jj Kk Ll Mm Nn

Unit 6

How many _____ do you have?

1  car**s**	2 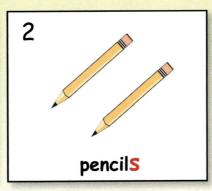 pencil**s**	3 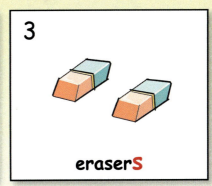 eraser**s**
4 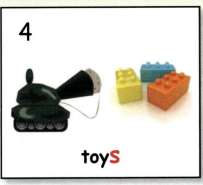 toy**s**	5 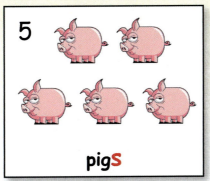 pig**s**	6  friend**s**

I have...

Listening Practice

Practice as a class and then ask each student individually without any gestures. Sign or stamp when the student can respond correctly to all of the questions or commands.

1. How many pencils do you have?
2. What is this?
3. Do you like this game?
4. Where is your textbook?
5. How many friends do you have?

Sign or Stamp

Count and write the number in the boxes. Color.

1. How many chickens are there?

2. How many rabbits are there?

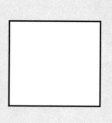 

3. How many dogs are there?

1. Practice as a class. 2. Practice individually. 3. Sign or stamp only when the student can read it on their own without help.

at

as

an

ad

Sign or Stamp

Students can work on this while you test them one on one on the previous page.

Mm Nn Oo Pp Qq Rr Ss

Tt Uu Vv Ww Xx Yy Zz

1. Practice as a class. 2. Practice individually. 3. Sign or stamp only when the student can read it on their own without help.

I am at an app.

Sign or Stamp

Students can work on this while you test them one on one on the previous page.

Unit 7

Common Classroom English

Students should be able to understand these and say them individually without help.

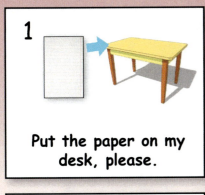

1. Put the paper on my desk, please.

2. Put the paper on the shelf, please.

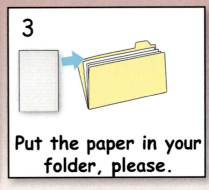

3. Put the paper in your folder, please.

4. Close the door, please.

5. Open the door, please.

6. You need to say sorry.

Listening Practice

Practice as a class and then ask each student individually without any gestures. Sign or stamp when the student can respond correctly to all of the questions or commands.

1. Put the paper on my desk, please.
2. Put the book on the shelf, please.
3. Open the door, please.
4. Where is your textbook?
5. What is your name?
6. Close the door, please.

Sign or Stamp

1. Get the car to the finish line.
2. Write the sentence beautifully.

The car is fast.

1. Practice as a class. 2. Practice individually. 3. Sign or stamp only when the student can read it on their own without help.

cat	can
bat	fan
hat	tan
fat	ban

Sign or Stamp

Sign or Stamp

Students can work on this while you test them one on one on the previous page.

cats   1.   2.

bat   1.   2.

42

1. Practice as a class. 2. Practice individually. 3. Sign or stamp only when the student can read it on their own without help.

A fat cat is on a mat.

Sign or Stamp

Students can work on this while you test them one on one on the previous page.

Unit 8

Classroom English

Listening Practice

Practice as a class and then ask each student individually without any gestures. Sign or stamp when the student can respond correctly to all of the questions or commands.

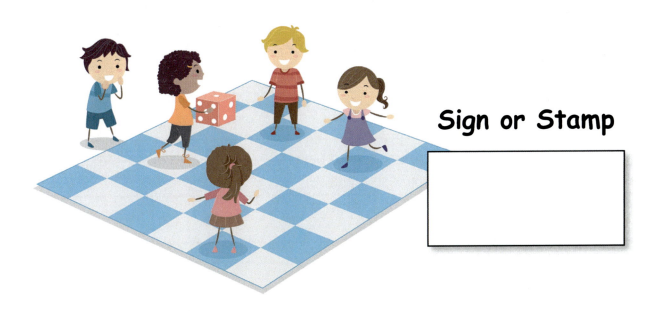

Sign or Stamp

1. Get the cat to the milk.
2. Write the sentence beautifully.

The cat gets milk.

1. Practice as a class. 2. Practice individually. 3. Sign or stamp only when the student can read it on their own without help.

sag	ram
rag	ham
tag	Sam
bag	dam

Sign or Stamp

Sign or Stamp

Students can work on this while you test them one on one on the previous page.

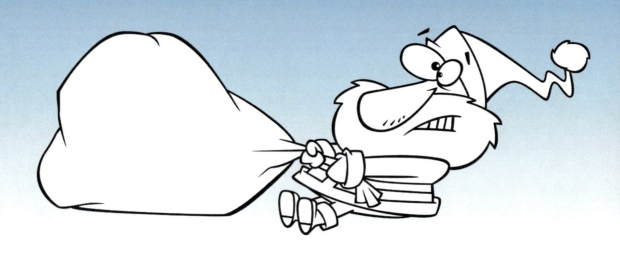

1.   2.

bag _____

1.   2.

ram _____

1. Practice as a class. 2. Practice individually. 3. Sign or stamp only when the student can read it on their own without help.

Sam has a ham.

Sign or Stamp

Students can work on this while you test them one on one on the previous page.

Review Assessments

A. Speaking

1. Practice as a class and in partners beforehand.
2. How many sentences can you make in a minute?

1. (question) 3. (question) 5. (question) 7. (question)
2. (answer)   4. (answer)   6. (answer)   8. (answer)

9. (question) 11. (question) 13. (question) 15. (question)
10. (answer)   12. (answer)   14. (answer)   16. (answer)

  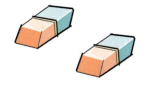 

17. 18. 19. 20.

 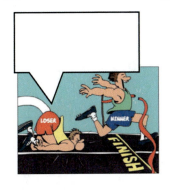  #1   #2

Review Assessments

B. Reading

How many letters and sounds can the student do in a minute? (Start over at 1 if the student finishes the list before a minute has passed.)

1.	2.	3.	4.	5.	6.	7.	8.
u	e	a	i	o	y	z	b
9.	10.	11.	12.	13.	14.	15.	16.
r	p	q	w	x	v	b	k
17.	18.	19.	20.	21.	22.	23.	24.
d	g	j	h	n	m	f	i

C. Listening

Ask each student individually without gestures of any kind. How many questions out of the total does the student respond correctly to?

1. Where is the car?
2. How many pencils do you have?
3. Open the door, please.
4. What is your name?
5. Put the paper on my desk, please.
6. Where is your textbook?
7. Put the textbook on the shelf, please.
8. Do you like this game?
9. How many friends do you have?
10. What is this?

D. Vocabulary

See how many words the student can remember out of the total.

1.
2.
3.
4.
5.
6.
7.

8.
9.
10.
11.
12.
13.
14.

Unit 9

Classroom English

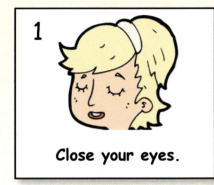
1. Close your eyes.

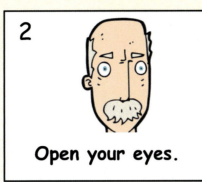
2. Open your eyes.

3. Raise your hand.

4. Touch your knees.

5. Crawl on the floor.

6. Turn around.

Listening Practice

Practice as a class and then ask each student individually without any gestures. Sign or stamp when the student can respond correctly to all of the questions or commands.

Sign or Stamp

1. Get the boy to the dog.
2. Write the sentence beautifully.

The kid and dog play.

1. Practice as a class. 2. Practice individually. 3. Sign or stamp only when the student can read it on their own without help.

dot
lot
pot
hot

cop
top
mop
hop

Sign or Stamp

Sign or Stamp

Students can work on this while you test them one on one on the previous page.

hot   1. _____   2. _____

dogs   1. _____   2. _____

1. Practice as a class. 2. Practice individually. 3. Sign or stamp only when the student can read it on their own without help.

The cop is on top.

Sign or Stamp

Students can work on this while you test them one on one on the previous page.

Unit 10

Classroom English

Do you have a _____?

1. cold

2. snack

3. ruler

4. coat

5. sweater

6. hat

Listening Practice

Practice as a class and then ask each student individually without any gestures. Sign or stamp when the student can respond correctly to all of the questions or commands.

1. How are you?
2. Do you have a cold?
3. Where is your pencil?
4. Sit properly.
5. Close your eyes.
6. Touch your knees.
7. Do you have a snack?

Sign or Stamp

1. Find the differences.
2. Write the sentence beautifully.

The dog can jump.

1. Practice as a class. 2. Practice individually. 3. Sign or stamp only when the student can read it on their own without help.

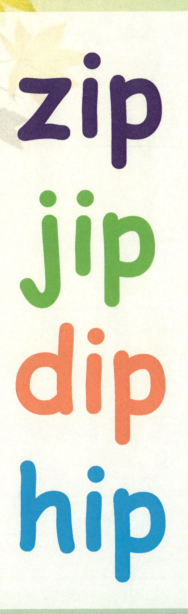

Sign or Stamp

Sign or Stamp

Students can work on this while you test them one on one on the previous page.

hit   1.   2.

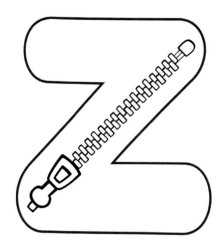

zip   1.   2.

1. Practice as a class. 2. Practice individually. 3. Sign or stamp only when the student can read it on their own without help.

He has a fix-it kit.

Sign or Stamp

Students can work on this while you test them one on one on the previous page.

Unit 11

Classroom English

Do you have a _____ at home?

1  rabbit	2  bear	3 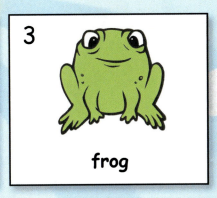 frog
4  fish	5  lizard	6  dinosaur

Common Mistake

A common mistake for Asian speakers learning English is to say "My home have...". If your students have this problem, have them correct you when you say it wrong.

Sign or Stamp

1. Help the bunny get to the egg.
2. Write the sentence beautifully.

It will get the egg.

1. Practice as a class. 2. Practice individually. 3. Sign or stamp only when the student can read it on their own without help.

big	win
pig	fin
wig	tin
dig	bin

Sign or Stamp

Sign or Stamp

Students can work on this while you test them one on one on the previous page.

pig

1.   2.

fin

1.   2.

1. Practice as a class. 2. Practice individually. 3. Sign or stamp only when the student can read it on their own without help.

The big pig wins!

Sign or Stamp

Students can work on this while you test them one on one on the previous page.

Unit 12

Classroom English

I am _____.

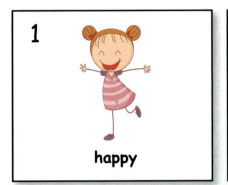
1 happy

2 sad

3 angry

4 hungry

5 thirsty

6 sick

Speaking Practice

Act out the different pictures above and the students should be able to say the correct sentence.

Sign or Stamp

1. Help the pirate get to the boat.
2. Write the sentence beautifully.

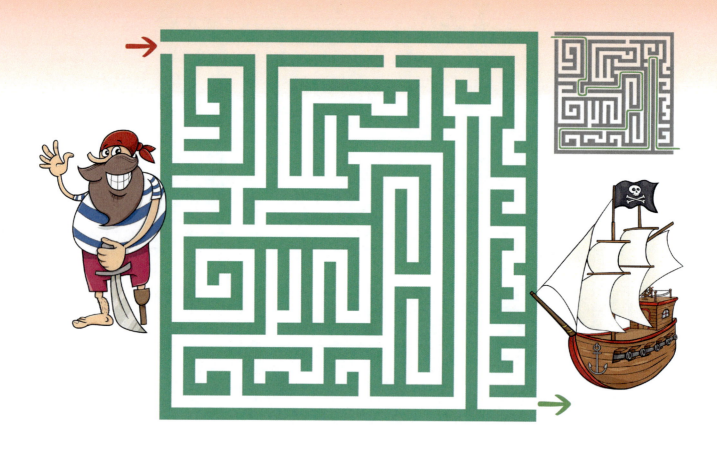

The man is not sad.

1. Practice as a class. 2. Practice individually. 3. Sign or stamp only when the student can read it on their own without help.

hug
bug
rug
tug

bun
sun
fun
run

Sign or Stamp

Sign or Stamp

Students can work on this while you test them one on one on the previous page.

1.   2.

bug

1.   2.

run

1. Practice as a class. 2. Practice individually. 3. Sign or stamp only when the student can read it on their own without help.

It gets the bug.

Sign or Stamp

Students can work on this while you test them one on one on the previous page.

Review Assessments

A. Speaking

1. Practice as a class and in partners beforehand.
2. How many sentences can you make in a minute?

1.
2.
3. (question)
4. (answer)

5. (question)
6. (answer)

7. (question)
8. (answer)

9. (question)
10. (answer)
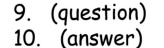
11. (question)
12. (answer)

13. (question)
14. (answer)

15. (question)
16. (answer)

17. (question)
18. (answer)
19. (question)
20. (answer)

21. (question)
22. (answer)

77

Review Assessments

B. Reading

How many words can the student read in a minute? (Start over at 1 if the student finishes the list before a minute has passed.)

1. cat	2. bag	3. ram	4. hot	5. dog	6. cop
7. hit	8. dip	9. win	10. big	11. fat	12. rot
13. sag	14. top	15. pig	16. lit	17. log	18. nag

C. Listening

Ask each student individually without gestures of any kind. How many questions out of the total does the student respond correctly to?

1. Close your eyes.
2. Touch your knees.
3. Open your eyes.
4. Raise your hand.
5. Crawl on the floor.
6. Turn around.
7. Do you have a cold?
8. Do you have a dinosaur?
9. How are you?
10. How old are you?

D. Vocabulary

See how many words the student can remember out of the total.

Unit 13

What color is it?
It is _____.

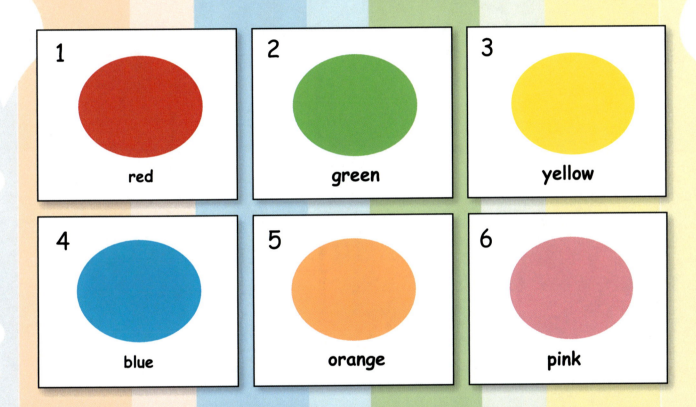

Speaking Practice

Ask each student individually about the colors of different objects. Sign or stamp only when the student can do it by him or herself.

Sign or Stamp

1. Help the pirate get to the boat.
2. Write the sentence beautifully.

The dog can get him.

1. Practice as a class. 2. Practice individually. 3. Sign or stamp only when the student can read it on their own without help.

hut	sub
cut	rub
but	hub
nut	cub

Sign or Stamp

Sign or Stamp

Students can work on this while you test them one on one on the previous page.

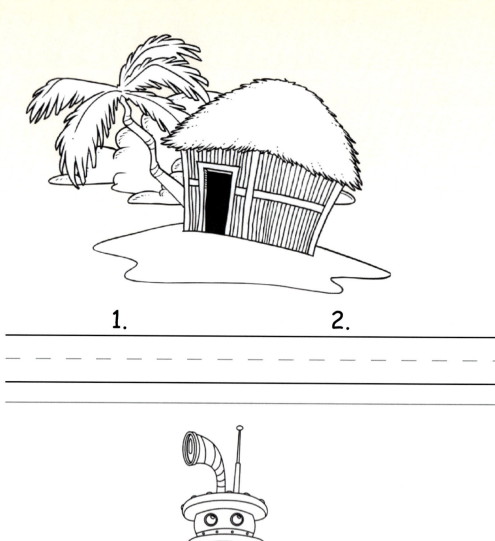

hut   1. _____   2. _____

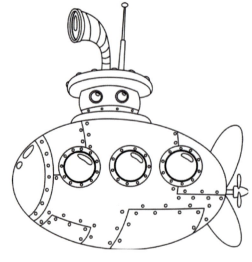

sub   1. _____   2. _____

1. Practice as a class. 2. Practice individually. 3. Sign or stamp only when the student can read it on their own without help.

The cub has a hut.

Sign or Stamp

Students can work on this while you test them one on one on the previous page.

84

Unit 14

What color is it?
It is _____.

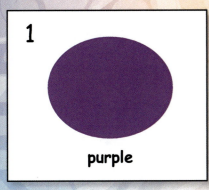
1 purple

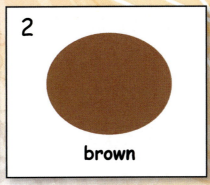
2 brown

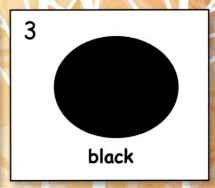
3 black

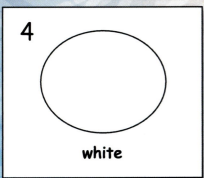
4 white

5 light blue

6 dark blue

Speaking Practice
Ask each student individually about the colors of different objects. Sign or stamp only when the student can do it by him or herself.

Sign or Stamp

1. Help the pirate get to the boat.
2. Write the sentence beautifully.

It can run fast.

1. Practice as a class. 2. Practice individually. 3. Sign or stamp only when the student can read it on their own without help.

yet	tex
vet	rex
met	pen
let	hen

Sign or Stamp

Sign or Stamp

Students can work on this while you test them one on one on the previous page.

1. 2.

T-rex

1. 2.

vet

1. Practice as a class. 2. Practice individually. 3. Sign or stamp only when the student can read it on their own without help.

The vet gets to the pets.

Sign or Stamp

Students can work on this while you test them one on one on the previous page.

Unit 15

Review the numbers and do the listening test while students do the next page.

11	12	13
14	15	16
17	18	19
20		

Listening Test

Can the student point to the numbers the teacher says?

Sign or Stamp

1. Can you get the student to the end?
2. Write the sentence beautifully.

I can do it!

1. Practice as a class. 2. Practice individually. 3. Sign or stamp only when the student can read it on their own without help.

bed	get
red	pet
Ned	jet
fed	set

Sign or Stamp

Sign or Stamp

Students can work on this while you test them one on one on the previous page.

bed ___1._____2._____

pet ___1._____2._____

1. Practice as a class. 2. Practice individually. 3. Sign or stamp only when the student can read it on their own without help.

It sets a jet on its back.

Sign or Stamp

Students can work on this while you test them one on one on the previous page.

Review Assessments

A. Speaking

1. Practice as a class and in partners beforehand.
2. How many sentences can you make in a minute?

1.

2.

3.

4.

5.

6. (question)
7. (answer)

8. (question)
9. (answer)

10. (question)
11. (answer)

12.

13. #1

14. #2

15.

97

Review Assessments

B. Reading

How many words can the student read in a minute? (Start over at 1 if the student finishes the list before a minute has passed.)

1. cup   2. hat   3. tin   4. red   5. rub   6. cop

7. get   8. bit   9. bag   10. top   11. hit   12. hut

13. hot   14. tap   15. pig   16. bed   17. fun   18. has

C. Listening

Ask each student individually without gestures of any kind. How many questions out of the total does the student respond correctly to?

1. Hi, how are you?
2. What is your name?
3. How old are you?
4. What do you like to eat?
5. How many pencils do you have?
6. Are you sick?
7. Do you have a cold?
8. Do you have a cat at home?
9. What color is it?
10. Close your eyes.

D. Vocabulary

See how many words the student can remember out of the total.

1. (red)   2. (green)   3. (blue)   4. (orange)   5. (yellow)   6. (pink)   7. (black)

8. (brown)   9. (purple)   10. (white)   11. (light blue)   12. (dark blue)   13. 11   14. 12

Copyright 2021
Kid-Inspired Classroom

All rights reserved. No part of this book may be reproduced in any form.

Made in the USA
Middletown, DE
30 August 2024